THE IMPACT OF SOCIAL MEDIA ON

MENTAL HEALTH AND WELL-BEING

WRITTEN

BY

AHIAKWO MIRACLE

TABLE OF CONTENT

COPYRIGHT

DEDICATION:

This book is dedicated to all those who have been impacted by social media on their mental health and well-being. May the insights and techniques shared in this book help you navigate the complexities of social media and find a healthy balance in your online and offline life.

CHAPTER 1: INTRODUCTION

Social media has become a ubiquitous part of our daily lives, with billions of people around the world using platforms such as Facebook, Twitter, Instagram, and TikTok to connect with friends and family, share photos and videos, and express their thoughts and opinions. While social media has undoubtedly brought many benefits, including increased social connectedness and access to information, there is growing concern about the impact that these platforms may be having on our mental health and well-being.

The purpose of this book is to explore the complex relationship between social media and mental health. We will examine both the positive and negative effects that social media can have on our psychological well-being, as well as the potential for addiction and the strategies that individuals can use to manage their social media use. Additionally, we will look to the future to consider how social media may continue to evolve and how these changes may impact our mental health.

As we delve into this topic, it is important to acknowledge that social media is not inherently good or bad. Rather, it is a tool that can be used in a variety of ways, and its effects on mental health are likely to be influenced by a range of factors, including individual differences, social context, and cultural norms. Moreover, the relationship between social media and mental health is complex and multifaceted, and there is still much that we do not fully understand.

Despite these complexities, there is growing evidence that social media use may be associated with a range of mental health outcomes, including depression, anxiety, and loneliness. For example, studies have found that individuals who spend more time on social media may be more likely to experience symptoms of depression and anxiety, and that the use of social media may be linked to feelings of social isolation and FOMO (fear of missing out).

However, it is also important to acknowledge that social media can have positive effects on mental health. For example, social media can provide a sense of social connectedness, particularly for individuals who may be isolated or marginalized in other ways. Social media can also be a source of emotional support and validation, as well as a platform for advocacy and activism.

As we navigate this complex landscape, it is important to approach the topic with an open mind and a willingness to critically evaluate the evidence. While it may be tempting to dismiss social media as inherently harmful or beneficial, the reality is likely to be much more nuanced. By taking a balanced and evidence-based approach, we can better understand the potential risks and benefits of social media use and develop strategies to ensure that we are using these platforms in ways that promote our mental health and well-being.

Throughout the rest of this book, we will explore the various ways that social media can impact our mental health, including the potential for addiction, the impact of social comparison and self-esteem, and the role of social support and community. We will also delve into the strategies that individuals can use to manage their social media use, such as setting boundaries and using mindfulness techniques.

Additionally, we will examine the ways in which social media may continue to evolve in the future and how these changes may impact our mental health. For example, the rise of virtual reality and augmented reality could fundamentally change the way that we interact with social media, potentially leading to new forms of addiction and social comparison.

Ultimately, our goal in writing this book is to provide readers with a comprehensive understanding of the complex relationship between social media and mental health. By exploring the

potential risks and benefits of social media use, as well as the

strategies that individuals can use to manage their use, we hope

to empower readers to make informed decisions about their

social media use and to promote their mental health and well-

being in a digital world.

CHAPTER 2: POSITIVE EFFECTS OF

SOCIAL MEDIA ON MENTAL HEALTH

While there is growing concern about the potential negative effects of social media on mental health, it is important to acknowledge that these platforms can also have positive effects on our psychological well-being. In this chapter, we will explore some of the ways that social media can benefit mental health and well-being.

1. Social Support:

One of the most well-documented benefits of social media is its ability to facilitate social support. Social media platforms provide individuals with a means to connect with others who share similar experiences, interests, and concerns. This can be particularly beneficial for individuals who may be isolated or marginalized in other ways, such as those living with chronic illnesses or disabilities.

Research has shown that social support received through social media can have a positive impact on mental health outcomes, including reducing symptoms of depression and anxiety. Social media can also be a source of emotional support, validation, and encouragement, which can help to enhance feelings of self-worth and improve overall psychological well-being.

2. Community Building

Social media can also facilitate community building, providing individuals with a sense of belonging and connection to a larger group. This can be particularly beneficial for individuals who may feel disconnected or alienated from their physical communities.

Social media can also be a platform for advocacy and activism, allowing individuals to connect with others who share their beliefs and values and to work together to effect change. This can provide individuals with a sense of purpose and meaning, which can enhance overall psychological well-being.

3. Access to Information and Resources

Social media can also provide individuals with access to

information and resources that can be beneficial for mental health and well-being. For example, social media can be a source of information about mental health conditions and treatment options, as well as a platform for connecting with mental health professionals and support organizations.

Additionally, social media can provide individuals with access to self-help resources and tools, such as meditation apps and mindfulness practices. These resources can help individuals to manage stress and anxiety, improve sleep, and enhance overall psychological well-being.

4. Positive Emotions

Finally, social media can also be a source of positive emotions, such as joy, humor, and inspiration. Social media platforms provide individuals with a means to connect with others who share their interests and passions, and to discover new ideas and perspectives.

Research has shown that exposure to positive emotions can have a range of benefits for mental health and well-being, including reducing symptoms of depression and anxiety and enhancing overall life satisfaction.

While it is important to acknowledge the potential risks of social media use, it is clear that social media can also have positive effects on mental health and well-being. By providing individuals with a means to connect with others, access information and resources, and experience positive emotions, social media can enhance overall psychological well-being and promote resilience in the face of stress and adversity.

It is important to note, however, that the positive effects of social media may be influenced by a range of factors, including individual differences, social context, and cultural norms. For example, the benefits of social support received through social media may depend on the quality of the support provided and the degree of similarity between the individual and their social network.

Additionally, the positive effects of social media may be more pronounced for individuals who use these platforms in a balanced and mindful way, rather than in a compulsive or addictive manner. As we will explore in later chapters, developing strategies for managing social media use and engaging with these platforms in a healthy and intentional way can be key to maximizing the potential benefits of social media while minimizing its potential risks.

Overall, while there is still much to learn about the complex relationship between social media and mental health, it is clear that social media can have positive effects on psychological well-being. By exploring these positive effects, we can develop a more nuanced and balanced understanding of how social media impacts mental health and well-being, and develop strategies for using these platforms in a way that promotes our overall psychological health and resilience.

CHAPTER 3: NEGATIVE EFFECTS OF SOCIAL MEDIA ON MENTAL HEALTH

While there are certainly positive aspects to social media use, there is also growing concern about the potential negative effects of these platforms on mental health and well-being. In this chapter, we will explore some of the ways that social media can have negative effects on mental health.

1. Social Comparison:

One of the most well-documented negative effects of social

media is its potential to foster social comparison. Social media platforms provide individuals with a constant stream of curated content from their friends, family, and acquaintances, which can lead to feelings of envy, inadequacy, and self-doubt.

Research has shown that exposure to idealized images and lifestyles on social media can contribute to negative body image, low self-esteem, and symptoms of depression and anxiety. Additionally, social comparison on social media can contribute to feelings of FOMO (fear of missing out), which can lead to compulsive checking and engagement with these platforms.

2. Cyberbullying

Another potential negative effect of social media is the risk of cyberbullying. Social media platforms provide individuals with a means to communicate and interact with others anonymously or from a distance, which can lead to a greater risk of harassment, bullying, and other forms of online abuse.

Cyberbullying can have profound effects on mental health, including increased symptoms of depression, anxiety, and post-traumatic stress disorder (PTSD). Additionally, cyberbullying can lead to social isolation and feelings of shame, which can further exacerbate mental health problems.

3. Addiction:

Social media addiction is a growing concern, with many individuals reporting compulsive use and difficulty disengaging from these platforms. Social media addiction can have negative effects on mental health, including increased symptoms of anxiety, depression, and sleep problems.

Additionally, social media addiction can lead to problems with impulse control and self-regulation, which can contribute to a range of negative outcomes, including academic and occupational problems, relationship difficulties, and financial problems.

4. Disrupted Sleep Patterns:

Finally, social media use can also disrupt sleep patterns, which can contribute to a range of mental health problems, including symptoms of depression, anxiety, and irritability. Exposure to blue light from electronic devices can suppress melatonin production, which can interfere with the natural sleep-wake cycle.

Additionally, engaging with stimulating or stressful content on social media before bed can make it difficult to relax and fall asleep, leading to sleep deprivation and daytime fatigue.

While social media can have negative effects on mental health, it is important to note that these effects may be influenced by a range of individual and contextual factors. For example, the negative effects of social comparison may be more pronounced for individuals who are already vulnerable to body image concerns or low self-esteem, while the negative effects of cyberbullying may depend on the severity and duration of the harassment.

Moreover, the negative effects of social media may be mitigated by developing strategies for managing social media use, such as setting boundaries, engaging in offline activities, and seeking support from mental health professionals or support groups.

Overall, while there are certainly negative aspects to social media use, it is important to acknowledge that these platforms are not inherently harmful and that their effects on mental health are likely to be complex and multifaceted. By exploring the potential negative effects of social media, we can develop a more nuanced and balanced understanding of how these platforms impact mental health and well-being, and develop strategies for minimizing the potential risks while maximizing the potential benefits of social media use.

CHAPTER 4: ADDICTION AND SOCIAL MEDIA

One of the most concerning potential negative effects of social media use is addiction. Social media addiction is a growing concern, with many individuals reporting compulsive use and difficulty disengaging from these platforms. In this chapter, we will explore the concept of social media addiction, its potential negative effects, and strategies for managing social media use.

1. What is Social Media Addiction?

Social media addiction is a behavioral addiction characterized by compulsive use of social media platforms despite negative consequences. Individuals with social media addiction may experience intense cravings to use these platforms, spend excessive amounts of time engaging with them, and struggle to disengage from them even when they want to.

Research suggests that social media addiction may be driven by a variety of factors, including the reward and reinforcement mechanisms built into these platforms, the fear of missing out on important information or social interactions, and the desire for social validation and connection.

2. Negative Effects of Social Media Addiction

Social media addiction can have a range of negative effects on mental health and well-being, including increased symptoms of anxiety, depression, and sleep problems. Additionally, social media addiction can lead to problems with impulse control and self-regulation, which can contribute to a range of negative outcomes, including academic and occupational problems, relationship difficulties, and financial problems.

Social media addiction can also exacerbate other mental health problems, such as social anxiety and body image concerns. For example, individuals with social anxiety may use social media as a means of avoiding face-to-face interactions, leading to a cycle of avoidance and isolation. Similarly, exposure to idealized images and lifestyles on social media can contribute to negative body image and low self-esteem.

3. Strategies for Managing Social Media Use

If you suspect that you may be struggling with social media addiction, there are several strategies that you can use to manage your use and promote your mental health and well-being. Some of these strategies include:

1. Setting boundaries: Establishing clear boundaries around your social media use, such as limiting your use to certain times of day or certain activities, can help you to regain control over your behavior and reduce the risk of compulsive use.

2. Engaging in offline activities: Focusing on offline activities, such as exercise, hobbies, or socializing with friends and family,

can provide you with alternative sources of stimulation and social connection, reducing your reliance on social media.

3. Practicing mindfulness: Mindfulness practices, such as meditation or deep breathing exercises, can help you to become more aware of your thoughts and feelings, increasing your ability to regulate your behavior and manage urges to use social media.

4. Seeking support: If you are struggling with social media addiction, it can be helpful to seek support from mental health professionals or support groups. These resources can provide you with guidance, coping strategies, and support as you work to manage your social media use and improve your mental health.

5. Using technological tools: There are a variety of technological

tools, such as apps and browser extensions, that can help you to manage your social media use. These tools can help you to track your use, set limits on your behavior, and reduce the distracting or stimulating features of social media platforms.

6. Taking breaks: Taking periodic breaks from social media can help you to reset your behavior and reduce the risk of addiction. Consider taking a day or a week off from social media, or limiting your use to certain times of day or certain activities.

By developing strategies for managing social media use, individuals can reduce the potential negative effects of addiction and promote their mental health and well-being. It is important to note, however, that social media addiction can be a complex and challenging issue to address. If you are struggling with social media addiction, it may be helpful to seek support from mental health professionals or support groups to develop a personalized

plan for managing your use.

CHAPTER 5: TECHNIQUES FOR

MANAGING SOCIAL MEDIA USE

Social media has become an integral part of our daily lives, and while it offers many benefits, it can also have negative effects on our mental health and well-being. It's important to find a balance between the benefits of social media and the potential harms. Here are some techniques for managing social media use:

1. Set limits on social media use

One of the best ways to manage social media use is to set limits on the amount of time spent on social media platforms. This can be done by setting a time limit for daily use or by designating specific times of the day to check social media. Some apps allow users to set time limits for social media use, which can be helpful for those who have trouble sticking to self-imposed limits.

2. Take breaks from social media

Taking regular breaks from social media can help to reduce the negative impact it can have on mental health. This could involve a social media detox for a few days or simply taking a break during the workday. By stepping away from social media, it's possible to re-focus on other aspects of life and reduce stress and anxiety.

3. Curate social media feeds

The content we consume on social media can have a significant impact on our mental health and well-being. Curating social media feeds to include content that is positive, inspiring, and uplifting can help to create a more positive experience on social media. Unfollowing or muting accounts that post negative or triggering content can also be helpful in reducing the impact of social media on mental health.

4. Foster real-world connections

While social media can help to keep us connected, it's important to foster real-world connections as well. Making time for in-person interactions with friends and family can help to reduce feelings of loneliness and isolation, which can be exacerbated by social media use. Joining clubs or interest groups can also be a great way to meet new people and expand social circles.

5. Practice mindfulness

Mindfulness involves being present in the moment and paying

attention to thoughts and feelings without judgment. This practice can be helpful in reducing the negative impact of social media on mental health. By practicing mindfulness, it's possible to become more aware of how social media use affects mental health and to take steps to reduce the negative impact.

6. Seek professional help

For those who are struggling with the negative effects of social media on mental health, seeking professional help may be necessary. A mental health professional can provide support and guidance in managing social media use and addressing any underlying mental health concerns that may be exacerbated by social media. This could involve therapy, counseling, or other forms of treatment.

7. Use social media for positive purposes

Social media can be used for positive purposes, such as connecting with loved ones, promoting self-expression, and supporting social causes. By using social media for positive purposes, it's possible to create a more meaningful and fulfilling experience on social media. This could involve sharing positive content, participating in online communities that align with personal values, or using social media to raise awareness about social issues.

Managing social media use is crucial in maintaining good mental health and well-being. By setting limits, taking breaks, curating social media feeds, fostering real-world connections, practicing mindfulness, seeking professional help, and using social media for positive purposes, it's possible to reduce the negative impact of social media on mental health and create a more positive experience online. It's important to find a balance between the benefits of social media and the potential harms, and to prioritize mental health and well-being in the use of social media.

CHAPTER 6: THE FUTURE OF SOCIAL MEDIA AND MENTAL HEALTH

Social media has had a significant impact on mental health and well-being, both positive and negative. As technology continues to evolve, it's important to consider the potential future impact of social media on mental health. Here are some potential developments and trends to consider:

1. Increased focus on mental health and well-being features

Many social media platforms have already started to incorporate mental health and well-being features, such as tools to manage screen time, options to hide negative comments, and resources for mental health support. In the future, we can expect to see even more emphasis on mental health and well-being features, such as personalized wellness plans, mental health check-ins, and resources for managing stress and anxiety.

2. Greater use of virtual reality and augmented reality

Virtual reality and augmented reality are rapidly advancing technologies that have the potential to transform social media experiences. These technologies could be used to create immersive and interactive social experiences that promote connection and well-being. For example, virtual reality could be used to create virtual support groups, while augmented reality could be used to promote mindfulness and relaxation.

3. Continued concerns about the impact of social media on mental health

Despite efforts to promote mental health and well-being on social media, there will likely continue to be concerns about the potential negative impact of social media on mental health. This could include issues such as cyberbullying, social comparison, and addiction. As social media continues to evolve, it will be important to address these concerns and find ways to mitigate the potential negative impact on mental health.

4. Increased use of artificial intelligence

Artificial intelligence (AI) is being increasingly integrated into social media platforms, and this trend is likely to continue in the future. AI could be used to create more personalized social media experiences that promote mental health and well-being. For example, AI could be used to recommend content that aligns with individual interests and values, or to identify potential triggers for mental health concerns and provide targeted support.

5. Greater awareness of the impact of social media on mental health

As more research is conducted on the impact of social media on mental health, we can expect to see greater awareness and understanding of these issues. This could lead to increased efforts to promote mental health and well-being on social media, as well as greater regulation and oversight of social media platforms.

Social media is a rapidly evolving technology that has had a significant impact on mental health and well-being. While there are concerns about the potential negative impact of social media on mental health , there are also opportunities to use social media to promote mental health and well-being. As technology continues to advance, it will be important to consider the potential future impact of social media on mental health and to find ways to promote positive experiences online. This could involve incorporating mental health and well-being features, using virtual and augmented reality to promote connection and well-being, addressing concerns about the negative impact of social media on mental health, using artificial intelligence to create more personalized experiences, and increasing awareness and understanding of these issues. By taking a proactive approach to promoting mental health and well-being on social media, we can create a more positive and supportive online environment for everyone.

CHAPTER 7: CONCLUSION

Social media has revolutionized the way we connect with one another and share information, but it has also had a significant impact on mental health and well-being. While social media can offer many benefits, such as promoting social connectedness and providing access to mental health support, it can also have negative effects, such as cyberbullying, social comparison, and addiction.

In this book, we have explored the positive and negative effects of social media on mental health, as well as techniques for managing social media use and potential future trends and developments. It's clear that social media is a complex and nuanced technology that can have both positive and negative impacts on mental health, and that finding a balance between the benefits and potential harms is crucial in promoting well-being.

As we move forward, it's important to continue to research and understand the impact of social media on mental health, and to find ways to promote positive experiences online. This could involve incorporating mental health and well-being features into social media platforms, using virtual and augmented reality to promote connection and well-being, addressing concerns about the negative impact of social media on mental health, using artificial intelligence to create more personalized experiences, and increasing awareness and understanding of these issues.

Ultimately, the impact of social media on mental health will depend on how we choose to use it. By taking a proactive approach to managing social media use and promoting mental health and well-being online, we can create a more positive and

supportive online environment for ourselves and for others.

Printed in Great Britain
by Amazon